See p. 72

5/82

WEBSTER GROVES PRESBYTERIAN
NURSERY SCHOOL

TABLE TOYS

A CREATIVE CURRICULUM FOR EARLY CHILDHOOD

Creative Associates, Inc.

The Creative Curriculum Series was originally
prepared under grant HEW-90-C-438
to "Celebration in Learning '76". It was
revised and completed under contract from
the Administration for Children, Youth and
Families HEW-105-78-1003.

The material presented in this series
represents the opinions and viewpoints of
the authors and not necessarily those of
the funding agency.

Published by
Creative Associates, Inc.
3201 New Mexico Avenue, N.W.
Suite 270
Washington, D.C. 20016

Distributed by
Gryphon House
P.O. Box 217
Mount Rainer, Maryland 20822

Library of Congress Catalogue Card Number: 79-52823
ISBN 0-934362-04-1 (volume 4)
ISBN 0-934362-00-9 (set)

ACKNOWLEDGMENTS

This Curriculum Manual grew out of a series of six
workshops designed for early childhood staff in 1976.
Diane Dodge had the major responsibility for the design and implementation of the workshops. The following people contributed to specific sections of the
workshops:

    Theresa Anderson - Attribute Blocks, Unifix Blocks
                          and Homemade Toys
    Margaret Dickman - Homemade Toys
    Deborah Frisby   - Racism in Toys
    Tawara Taylor   - Sexism in Toys

The task of recording the content of the workshops in
book form was assumed by Ginny Redish. Staff members
who contributed ideas and suggestions to the develop-
ment of the manual were Charito Kruvant, Mimi Tse and
Cheryl Jones. It was revised and edited in 1979 by
Diane Dodge. Kathy Niebo was responsible for graphics,
Marley Clevenger Beers for the cover design and Joanne
Cooney for typing and layout.

We especially want to thank all the participants in
the workshops who freely shared their concerns and
experiences in working with young children.

TABLE TOYS

Table of Contents

FOREWORD

This Early Childhood Curriculum Manual is one of four manuals based on approaches developed in "Celebration in Learning '76" (CIL), a research and demonstration program funded by the Office of Child Development (DHEW) in cooperation with the Washington, D.C. Bicentennial Commission. A primary objective of CIL was to design and pilot test in-service training workshops for early childhood personnel with a special emphasis on the utilization of space and materials in the classroom. The workshops showed how room arrangement can affect children's behavior and offered practical ideas for organizing and using materials with young children. The training offered in these workshops served to help teachers identify and learn ways to extend the basic social and cognitive skills children can gain by exploring materials and participating in activities associated with six classroom areas: Blocks, Table Toys, Art, House Corner, Books, Clay and Play Dough.

Following these workshops, the CIL staff developed four Early Childhood Curriculum Manuals: Blocks, Table Toys, Art and House Corner. The manuals, as completed and revised by the staff of Creative Associates in 1979, are based on the content presented in the workshops. They are intended to provide specific guidance in using materials and arranging the areas where materials are used. Theoretical information is presented in the context of practical approaches which teachers can use to foster intellectual, socio/emotional and physical development of children.

A Trainer's Guide is available for each of the manuals. The guides present a workshop approach and philosophy and offer suggestions on presenting each section of the Curriculum Manual in a workshop setting.

Two of the manuals, Bloques and Arte, are available in Spanish. These manuals cover the same subject areas as their English counterparts but the specific content is oriented to the learning styles and special interests of Spanish speaking children.

A companion Annotated Bibliography entitled Resource Materials for the Creative Curriculum has also been produced by the project. The bibliography offers a comprehensive review of articles and books focusing on the House Corner, Art, Blocks, Table Toys, Water, Sand, Books and Clay/Play Dough. A special feature of the bibliography is the inclusion of a set of criteria to assist teachers and parents in evaluating the racial and ethnic images projected in children's books.

-1-

INTRODUCTION

Table Toys, A Creative Curriculum is designed for adults who work with young children and who wish to expand their use of table toys in the classroom. The first chapter explores what we mean by "table toys" and outlines some of the problems teachers commonly face in using table toys in the classroom. Chapters II and III consider the impact of the physical environment on children's behavior and ability to learn and offer practical suggestions for arranging furniture and displaying materials in the Table Toy Area. The teacher's role in encouraging and structuring the use of table toys is examined in Chapters IV and V. Toys which are typically found in early childhood classrooms are discussed and specific activities suggested for each one. The last chapter contains instructions for making toys and discusses the value and implications of teacher-made materials. For those who wish to read more extensively on these topics, an annotated listing of articles and books on the Table Toy Area can be found in Resource Materials for the Creative Curriculum.

The Table Toy Curriculum Manual is intended to serve a variety of needs. For the individual reader (including teachers and parents), the Manual offers a chapter-by-chapter sequence of topics which may be read as a whole or selectively depending on the needs and interests of the reader. For center directors and others involved in training teachers and parents, the topics covered in the Manual can serve as the subject matter for a workshop or series of workshops. A Trainer's Guide giving specific suggestions for presenting each topic in a workshop setting is also available.

The content of this Manual is particularly appropriate for teachers who are working towards a Child Development Associate credential. The original workshops were designed to help teachers develop the CDA competencies as they relate to the Table Toy Area.

CHAPTER I

AN INTRODUCTION TO TABLE TOYS

Topics covered in this chapter:

I-1. What is a table toy?

I-2. Grouping table toys.

I-3. What children learn from table toys.

I-4. Problems with table toys.

Goals for this chapter:

1.   to think about different toys in order to define
       and group them.

2.   to consider what children can learn from playing
       with table toys.

3.   to list some difficulties table toys can cause in
       the classroom.

I-1. <u>What is a table toy?</u>

If you think about the phrase "table toys" and associate it with single words (without naming any actual toys), what comes to your mind? Teachers have mentioned words like:

- quiet

- games

- hands

- sitting.

"Table toys" are toys and games that children play with relatively quietly and usually while sitting down. Although we call these "table toys", there is no reason why they have to be used on a table. Many children prefer the floor and you'll see some suggestions for this in pictures in Chapter II.

There are many toys and games that could be included in a Table Toy Area. You might find it interesting to make a survey of the table toys available in your center or classroom to compare it to the following list.

Puzzles -
    wooden ones
    rubber insets
    two-piece cardboard ones
Sewing cards
Shape sorting box
Stack of colored rings
Nesting boxes
Lotto games
Domino cards

Lego
Tinker Toys
Table size blocks
Building bricks
Lincoln Logs

Beads and strings
Pegs and pegboards
Colored inch cubes
Unifix cubes
Parquetry or pattern blocks
Attribute Blocks

Your center may not have every one of these and quite possibly you
have table toys that are not on this list. This is a sample of the
kinds of toys and games we have in mind when we speak of table toys.
You may find that your list differs from ours for some special
reason such as the age of the children in your class. Teachers
agree that age is an important factor in deciding what to include
as a table toy. Adults who work with infants and toddlers find
that some of the toys on this list are too difficult for their
children. They might keep toys like:

● the sorting box

● the ring stack

● the nesting boxes

● some easy wooden puzzles (especially the ones which
    have handles on the pieces)

but they wouldn't put out Tinker Toys or Lincoln Logs. They would
also add items that are not as appropriate for older children such
as push and pull toys.

Some teachers of four and five-year-olds feel that their children
would not be interested in the stacking rings or the nesting boxes,
but others have found that older children find some imaginative uses
for these toys.

I-2. Grouping table toys.

Different toys develop different skills. Therefore, it is important
to have a variety of toys available.

It would be very useful for teachers to know just what the children
might learn from each toy they put out. One way to do this is to
play with it yourself for a while. On the next page there are
some questions you may find helpful to think about when you are
looking at a toy.

Grouping Table Toys

1. What senses does the child use when working with this particular toy?
    (hearing, seeing, touching, smelling, tasting)

2. Type of toy:

    a. Is it a "self-correcting structured" toy? (That is, a toy which fits together in a certain way so the children know when they have finished and when they have done it correctly.)

    b. Or is it "open-ended"? (That is, a toy that can be put together in many different ways so that each time a child plays with it, something new can be made.)

    c. If it is open-ended, would it be used mostly for making buildings or for making patterns? What else might it be used for?

3. Which concepts or skills could be learned from this toy?
    (Examples would be: color, shape, number, balance, size order, same/different, and so on.)

4. What age group do you think this toy would be for?

5. What do you like (dislike) about this toy? What would
    children like (dislike) about it?

            <u>Adults:</u>   <u>Children:</u>

    Like: Like:

    Dislike: Dislike:

There are a number of different ways we could group table toys. The form just presented suggests several categories by which toys can be grouped:

(1) by the concepts that can be learned from them

(2) by the age-group they are meant for

(3) by the type of toy - self-correcting, open-ended, construction toys and pattern toys.

This division will be useful in selecting materials (Chapter III) and in discussing the teacher's role (Chapter V, especially Sections V-3 and V-4).

There is a fourth possible group that is not included in this list but that some teachers do include with table toys. These might be called "dramatic play" table toys such as:

- miniature size people

- small animals

- small size furniture

- community workers figures.

These are often used as accessories in the Block Area. They could also be used by themselves for quiet fantasy play or as accessories to table top construction toys.

I-3. <u>What children learn from table toys.</u>

We want our children to have fun at school and also to learn - to grow physically, mentally and socially. How do table toys help children learn?

Look over the list in the last section and think about what skills a child would be learning from these toys. You might enjoy playing with a few yourself to see what concepts and skills are involved. Or watch carefully one day in class and write down what you think the children are learning from the table toys they are working with. You can use this space to jot down your ideas.

_____

_____

_____

_____

_____

_____

Table toys can

- develop small muscle control

- develop eye-hand coordination

- develop visual skills and the sense of touch

- foster self-confidence because they give the children a chance to be successful by themselves

- give children a chance to work quietly.

They can help children learn

- to work by themselves

- to work together in small groups

- specific concepts such as color, number, size, shapes

- thinking skills like matching, patterning, sequencing, one-to-one correspondence, which are needed for learning reading and arithmetic

- the satisfaction of staying at a task until it is done.

You may have thought of other ways table toys help children learn. These are only some of the many reasons for including table toys in an early childhood curriculum.

I-4. Problems with table toys.

Many teachers have some concerns or worries about their Table Toy Area and how children use the toys. Some of the problems teachers commonly mention are:

- not enough storage space

- children don't clean up

- pieces get lost

- children take pieces home

- pieces get taken to other areas - as food in the House Corner, as decoration for clay or play dough projects

- when puzzle pieces are lost, the puzzle can't be used anymore

- children use toys as weapons

- children chew on pieces

- paper pieces get bent

- the game boxes get broken

- children fight over the toys and won't share

- children are bored, their interest span is short, there isn't enough variety

- children don't know what to do with the toys, they misuse them and break them

- table toys need a lot of teacher time and attention.

Do any of the concerns match yours? In the course of this book, we will deal with each of these problems. We hope you'll also find helpful suggestions for coping with other problems you may have with table toys.

Arranging the room and the toys so that the children know where materials belong can help with several of the items on this list. In the next two chapters, we look at room arrangement and how to display materials in the Table Toy Area.

CHAPTER II

ARRANGING SPACE FOR TABLE TOYS

Topics in this chapter:

II-1.   Behavior which has a negative/positive effect on learning.

II-2.   How room arrangement affects behavior - looking at different floor plans.

II-3.   Setting up a Table Toy Area.

Goals for this chapter:

1.   to think about how children's actions affect learning.

2.   to link behavior with room arrangements.

3.   to notice how different arrangements foster different behavior.

4.   to get some ideas for arranging an area for table toys that encourages positive behavior in children.

Introduction.

The physical environment has a great deal to do with how people act. When the chairs in a room are lined up against the wall separate from each other, people tend to sit alone, not talking together. If the chairs in the same room are grouped in circles around small tables, people begin to socialize more. The whole room takes on a happier, friendlier atmosphere. Just because the furniture has been moved, people act differently.

Before we can decide what room arrangements would be best in early childhood classrooms, however, we first have to think about how we want the children to behave. Then we can look at different ways to organize the furniture and consider how these arrangements might affect children's behavior.

II-1. Behavior which has a negative/positive effect on learning.

Think about a child who does well in your group. What is it about that child's behavior that helps him or her learn?

_____

_____

_____

_____

Some of the characteristics of positive behavior which teachers mention include:

- using materials well and taking care of them

- working at something until its finished

- being able to choose something to do

- being able to work alone

- being willing to share

- not being easily distracted by what others are doing

- showing curiosity, interest, asking questions, having ideas.

II-2. <u>How room arrangement affects behavior - looking at floor plans.</u>

Here is the plan of a pre-school classroom:

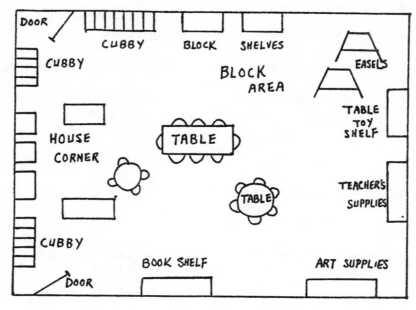

Figure 1

What do you notice about this room? What behavior do you think you would probably see here: Look in particular at the tables and shelves for table toys.

_____

_____

_____

_____

You may have noticed that:

● the tables are a long way from the toys. It is easy for the children to be distracted by other areas they have to pass by. The long walk back to the shelf probably discourages the children from cleaning up.

- the tables are out in the open. Children working with table toys can see everything else that is going on in the room. This may make it hard to concentrate on a table toy task.

- there is only one set of tables for both table toys and art activities. If both activities are available at the same time

  - the table toys may get covered with paint or glue

  - pieces of table toys may end up in the art work

  - children working on a table toy task may get distracted by the art activities.

In the room pictured in Figure 1, you would probably see

- a lot of aimless wandering

- a lot of running around

- children who are easily distracted and who change activities without completing anything

- toys left out, not cleaned up.

Now let's look at a different plan of the same space.

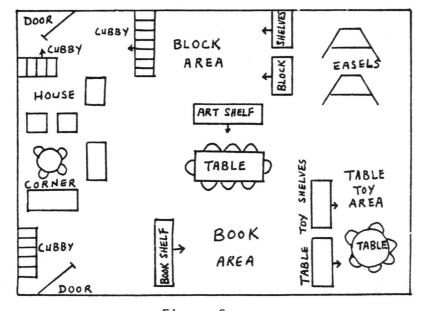

Figure 2

The same furniture has been rearranged. Concentrating again on
the table toys and the tables, think about what differences these
changes might make in what happens and in how the children behave.

_____

_____

_____

_____

In this arrangement:

- the table toy shelves have been moved away from the
  wall. Now they enclose a space with a table on the
  inside. This becomes a "Table Toy Area." A defined
  space helps children learn what materials and
  activities belong in that part of the room.

  Enclosed areas often help to give children a warm,
  secure feeling. Some children find it difficult to
  choose any activity in a large, open space.
  Enclosed spaces are smaller spaces, more suitable
  for the young child who can only cope with so
  much at one time.

- table toys are now separated from the art supplies and
  the Art Area. Table toys will be less likely to get
  mixed with art activities.

- the table toys are near the table. This should make
  it easier for the children to put the toys back. And
  there is less chance of a child's being distracted
  on the way to get or return a toy.

- the table toys are more removed from the noise of
  the other activities. Children would probably find
  it easier to concentrate on a task with this
  arrangement.

If you return to the beginning of this chapter where we listed
characteristics of behavior which encourage learning, you can see
that a separate, enclosed Table Toy Area where the toys are near
the table makes it easier for the children to

- choose an activity

- be independent

- stay at a task

- clean up by themselves.

The pictures in the next section show some more ideas for arranging your Table Toy Area.

II-3. <u>Setting up a Table Toy Area.</u>

1. In many preschool rooms, the shelves are all against the wall with the tables in front. This open arrangement makes is difficult to concentrate which is important in table toy activities.

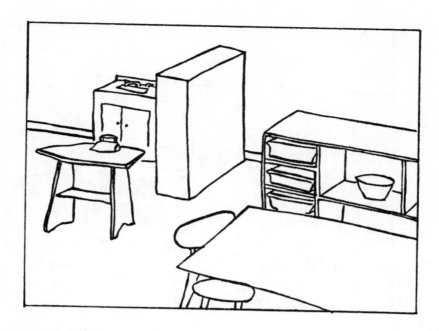

2.   Moving a shelf perpendicular to the wall sets one area off from the next but still leaves the table open to the distractions of the rest of the room.

3.   Using two shelves in an L shape and putting the table inside the enclosed space makes a more separate area. Children are less likely to run in and out of an area that is self-contained like this one.

4. It isn't enough just to tell the children with words that you want them to use materials in a certain place and a certain way. The children get messages from the furniture too. What do you think children are likely to do when they find this doll bed in front of the table toy shelf?

5. Here we find table toys on the House Corner stove. Putting the Table Toy Area right next to the House Corner can lead to misuse of toys. If children want pretend objects to cook, you can keep a supply of odds and ends (for example, styrofoam packing bits) in a container in the "kitchen". In addition, the noise from the House Corner may disturb children working at table toys.

6. Putting the Table Toy Area next to the Book Corner and the Art Area keeps the quiet activities together. It can be difficult for children to work on table toys if they are right next to noisy activities like block building or woodworking.

7. Children often prefer to use table toys on the floor. In an enclosed area they won't be disturbed by other children (if you leave enough room in the Table Toy Area itself).

8. You don't even need to have a table in the area at all. Rug
scraps set on the floor will define work spaces for individual
children. This will also keep children from getting in each
other's way or sitting too close to the shelves.

Once you've decided where to put your Table Toy Area, the next
step is what materials belong there and how to set them out.
That is the subject of the next chapter.

CHAPTER III

SELECTING AND DISPLAYING TABLE TOYS

Topics in this chapter:

III-1. Guidelines for selecting table toys.

III-2. Displaying materials in the classroom.

III-3. Caring for table toys.

Goals for this chapter:

1.   to establish some criteria for choosing table toys.

2.   to get specific ideas on displaying table toys and on labelling shelves.

3.   to learn how to make new puzzle pieces and how to make paper games more durable.

III-1. Guidelines for choosing table toys.

If you had to select table toys for your group of children, what would you think about when you made your choices? You might want to read over the first three sections of Chapter I again as you think about this question.

_____

_____

_____

_____

Most teachers say they want materials that are fun, challenging but not frustrating. Because children in any classroom have different interests and skills, teachers need to have a variety of toys available. A selection might include:

- some toys that children can do by themselves (self-correcting)

- some toys/games that a few children can do together

- some put-together toys that let children make their own constructions

- some "open-ended, pattern type" toys.

There are also several other factors that teachers have said they think about when choosing their table toys. These include:

- price

- durability

- attractiveness

- safety

- flexibility (has lots of uses)

- if it can be easily made

- age of the children

- experiences children have had before with this type of material

- do the materials include pictures of both men and women?

- whether the materials include pictures of both men and women as well as people from different racial and cultural groups.

For example, if you were considering whether or not to buy pegs and pegboards, you might go down this list and consider:

- price - not very expensive

- durability - they last a long time

- attractiveness - they come in bright colors

- safety - the small ones might not be good for toddlers who still put things in their mouths

- flexibility - they have many uses (i.e., making and/or following patterns)

- easily homemade - no

- age of children - not appropriate for children under two

- experience - children don't need experience to have fun with pegs

- sexism - not applicable

- racism - not applicable

- pegs can be fun, challenging (the small ones may be frustrating for children under two years).

Looking over this list of factors to consider in choosing a toy, most teachers would decide that pegs are a good investment for an early childhood classroom unless the teacher already has many pattern type toys or unless the children are all so young that the teacher has to worry about pegs being eaten. The guidelines can be used in a similar fashion to help you evaluate any toy or game you are considering for your classroom.

III-2. Displaying materials in the classroom.

How you display the toys and games in the classroom has an impact on
how they are used. The pictures on the next several pages should
give you some ideas to think about when you are setting out your
table toys. Many of the problems brought up in Section 4 of
Chapter I (Problems with table toys) are dealt with in these
pictures.

9. High cluttered shelves like this one make play difficult for
the children. It is hard for them to choose because it is
difficult to see what the choices are. Children may be uninten-
tionally destructive because they pull out the materials trying
to get to something they want.

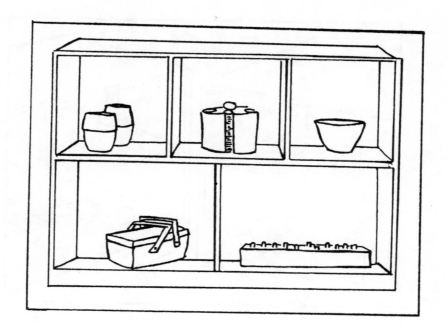

10. When toys are displayed so they can be seen clearly, children are more likely to use them. The children can take only the toy they want without messing up other materials.

11. This center has unit blocks and table toys together on the same shelf. What message is this giving to children?

12. Only toys that you want to be used in the Table Toy Area should be on the table toy shelves.

13. Messy shelves do not encourage children to be neat. When teachers leave the toys like this, children feel that it is OK just to throw everything on the shelf at clean-up time. It is easy to lose pieces this way.

14. If teachers put out broken toys and puzzles with pieces missing, the children won't be able to finish a task. Playing with incomplete table toys is not a satisfying experience. If teachers don't care about the materials, the children won't learn to take care of them either. (There are suggestions for maintaining table toys, including how to make new puzzle pieces, in the next section of this chapter.)

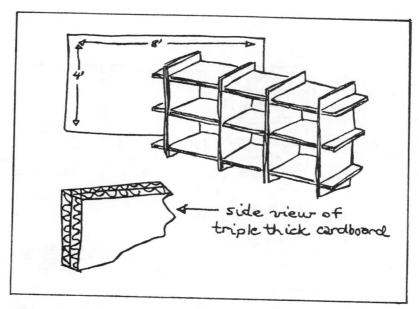

side view of triple thick cardboard

15. If we want children to be independent, the table toys should be out where they can be seen. Some teachers keep all the table toys stored away and only bring out a small selection each day. This makes work for the teacher and deprives the children of the chance to make choices by themselves. If you don't have enough furniture and money is scarce, shelves can be home-made inexpensively from sheets of tri-wall cardboard or boards and cinder blocks.

16. If the display shelves are neat, the children get the message that you expect the toys to be put back neatly. The physical appearance of the area is often a stronger influence on what children do than words would be. This display is neat but if all the toys are off the shelves, there is no clear way to know where to put toys back.

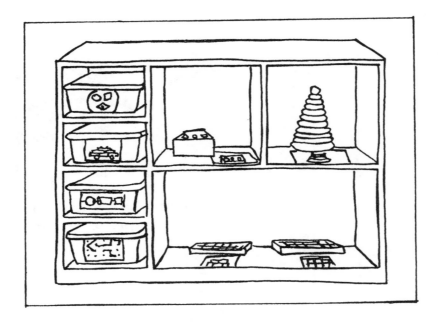

17. Labelling the shelves gives every toy or game its own place. Clean-up becomes a matching game - a skill-learning time instead of a chore. If the labels are pictures, the children can clean up by themselves without much help from the teacher. It's easy to see at a glance if any pieces are missing.

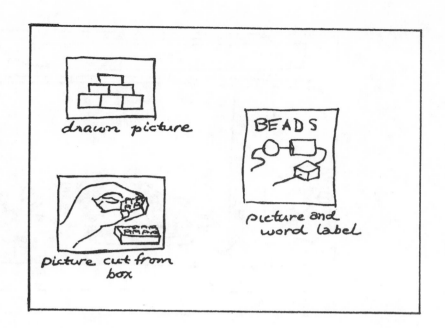

18. Labels are not difficult to make. You can cut a picture off the packaging from a new toy or from a toy catalogue, or you can draw one on heavy paper (white cardboard). It doesn't have to be very artistic just as long as the children recognize which toy is being shown. For older children, you can write the name next to the picture. If you cover the cardboard with clear adhesive paper (like transparent Contact), the label will last a long time. Stick it to the shelf with masking tape. When you rotate toys, just take the label off the shelf, store it with the toy, and it will be ready to put back on the shelf the next time you want to bring that toy out.

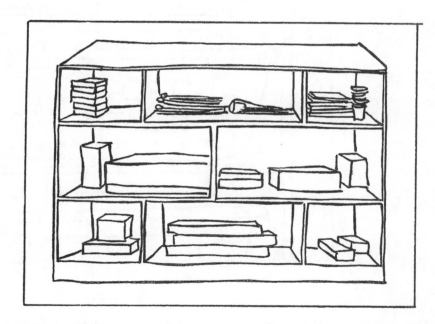

19. Closed boxes are not very attractive or inviting. The boxes break from being opened a lot. It is often hard for children to find the piece they want without dumping everything out of the box. Another reason for removing boxes is that the pictures on them are often racist and sexist. The children shown are almost always white. If girls are shown at all they are often watching while boys manipulate the toy. Removing the box eliminates those negative messages.

20. But just emptying the contents of the box on the shelf isn't a
very good solution. The shelves look messy and pieces get lost easily.

21. Some storage cabinets or shelves come with plastic bins but you can
buy inexpensive bins in any houseware department. Remember that labels
on each bin will help keep the different toys separated. Children can
easily see what is available and don't need to empty all the pieces onto
the table or floor.

III-3. <u>Caring for table toys.</u>

Among teachers' concerns that we listed in the first chapter were several related to caring for the toys, e.g., pieces disappear, paper parts get bent or chewed. For games with many pieces like pegs or beads, losing a few won't make much difference, but a puzzle with a missing part is very frustrating for children. You can fix puzzles in various ways:

(1) You can fill in the empty space with plaster of paris. If you paint it to match the background, the puzzle will be whole again, but will have one less piece to be put in.

(2) If you have a jig saw, you can make a new piece out of wood. Draw a pattern for the exact shape, cut it out, sand and paint to match the puzzle.

(3) You can remake small puzzle pieces by using plastic wood (also called wood putty). This mixture is flammable and gives off noxious fumes when it is being used, so it would be best to do this job away from the children and in a well-ventilated place. (Once it is dry, however, it is safe for the children to handle.) Lay plastic wrap in the empty hole where the missing piece goes. Pack wood putty in very tightly. Take out the plastic wrap filled with wood putty. Leave it to dry for three days.

When adults offer children broken toys, it conveys the message that the adults really don't care. Puzzles or other toys that cannot be completed unless all the pieces are there (matching games) should be considered "broken" whenever a piece is missing. They should be taken off the shelf until they are "fixed."

The durability of paper products is another problem many teachers share; but cardboard games like lotto or matching cards are inexpensive and useful table toys. Teachers can also make their own materials out of cardboard. You can preserve cardboard games in two ways:

(1) by dry-mounting and laminating the cards. This is a special process that requires a dry-mount machine; but if you have access to one, the techniques are easily learned.

(2) by using transparent adhesive backed paper (such as Contact paper) which you can buy by the yard in

houseware or hardware stores. Both of these make a
durable washable surface. While it takes some time
and work to do; once you have done it, you will have
toys and games that will last. If you use plastic
bins or cans for the materials that originally come
in paper boxes, you won't have the problem of losing
pieces because they fall out. The box cover can be
cut up to use as the label.

Most table toys can be washed with soap and water. Wooden pieces
should not be allowed to soak but should be dried quickly. An
occasional routine cleaning of all the table toys will increase
their attractiveness and help them to last a long time. It is
also an enjoyable class activity.

CHAPTER IV

SUPPORTING CHILDREN PLAYING WITH TABLE TOYS

Topics in this chapter:

IV-1. Setting rules.

IV-2. Using planning boards.

IV-3. Helping children who are using toys for the first time.

IV-4. Providing encouragement and teaching skills.

IV-5. Talking with children.

IV-6. Summary.

Goals for this chapter:

1.   to think about what the teacher can do in the Table Toy Area.

2.   to develop specific ideas for meeting the needs of individual children through the use of table toys.

Introduction.

The teacher who has thought about where to put the Table Toy Area, how to arrange the furniture, what toys to have in the room, and how to put them on the shelves has already done a big part of the job - preparing for table toy activities. In the next two chapters we talk about the teacher's role in working with the children.

Some teachers really enjoy the Table Toy Area. They feel comfortable working and playing with the children there. They find great satisfaction in watching a child complete a puzzle or helping a child to figure out how a toy goes together.

Other teachers are less sure of what their role should be. Often teachers would like more ideas for getting children interested in table toys and for sustaining their interest. In this chapter and the next one we will present ways the teacher can work both with children who have used table toys extensively and with children who are encountering table toys for the first time.

IV-1. Setting rules.

Children do respond to rules if they are simple, easily understood and reasonable. Rules are meant to make it easier for you and the children in your room to work well together. It is important for teachers who work as a team to sit down together and decide on what the rules are going to be. Children can deal with different sets of rules, for example at home and at school; but it would be very confusing to the children to have different rules in the same classroom.

Here are some possible rules for the Table Toy Area:

- table toys have to be used in the specified area

- toys may not be used as weapons

- toys have to be returned to their proper place when finished.

- only a certain number of children may use the Table Toy Area at one time (that number will depend on how many children can work comfortably in the space you have).

The rules should, of course, be explained to the children, but there are also ways to make rules easier for everyone to live by. We have already seen how room arrangement can help with rules about keeping table toys separate and about cleaning up. In Section IV-3 "Helping children who are using toys for the first time" we will give suggestions for children who have trouble sharing.

Crowding can also lead to problems. Activity areas should be large enough so that four or five children can work comfortably without getting in each other's way. How large you make the different areas has a lot to do with the way you set priorities about which activities are really important, how many children you want to be there at any one time and how much space you think a child needs to do that activity. All these are important ideas to consider when setting up your room and dividing up the space for the different activities.

If you have a very small room, one suggestion is to have different activities available at different times. For example, if you don't have enough space, a Quiet Area could be established and used for table toys at one time of day and art activities at a different time (or on different days). Curtains could be used to close off supplies you don't want used at any given time. Picture signs which are changed can indicate to the children what activity is available there at any given time.

IV-2. Using planning boards.

Planning boards are one way of helping children make a conscious choice of an area to play in and also of limiting the number of children who can play in that area at one time.

Planning boards can be made from pieces of pegboard or tri-wall and put up at the entrance to each activity center. Put as many pegs on the board as there are places in that area. (If five children can work comfortably at the toys and games, the planning board for the Table Toy Area should have five pegs.)

There should be a planning board for each activity area and all together there have to be at least as many pegs as there are children in the room. Each planning board should have a label (picture or picture-and-words) to show which area it is for.

Children in the class each have a personal card with a hole to go over the pegs. When they go into an area, the children hang their cards on the pegs of that planning board. Other children can see at a glance if there is more room. When children change areas, they also move their cards from one planning board to another.

Planning Boards

The children's personal cards become important symbols to them,
building positive self-concepts. For young children, you can use
a photo mounted on cardboard and laminated or covered with clear
(Contact adhesive backing) paper. Or you can use specific shapes.
The children quickly learn their own symbol and the other children's.
The same shape is used on the child's cubby, drinking cup, etc.
Learning this abstract representation is also a cognitive skill. For
older children you can use both name and symbol or just the child's
name.

Planning boards can help because

 ● they set limits to how many children can be in an area
    at one time without the teacher having to intervene.

 ● if an area doesn't get overcrowded, there are likely
    to be fewer sharing problems and less fighting.

 ● teachers who use planning boards find that there is
    less running around. Children tend to think more
    about where they want to work and to stay in an area
    longer. Children begin to plan how they will use
    their time.

 ● free choice is not inhibited by using planning boards.
    The children can still decide where they want to play
    and can change areas when they want to - as long as
    there is enough room there.

-36-

IV-3. <u>Helping children who are using toys for the first time.</u>

New experiences are always a bit scary. There are some specific ways adults can help.

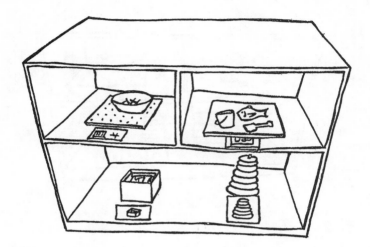

(1) One way to help is by the toys you select for the classroom. They should be simple and easy to do so that they are satisfying to the child with a short attention span. There should be some "self-correcting" ones and some "open-ended" ones (see Chapter I) that the children's small fingers can manage. A few suggestions might include:

- simple puzzles with large pieces and/or knobs

- stacking rings or nesting boxes

- pegs and pegboards

- large size Lego

- large beads and strings

- counting cubes.

What is important at this stage is to build up the child's self-confidence. A number of rewarding experiences at the toy table will probably make the child eager to try other, more challenging materials. Too many frustrating experiences may well cause the child to avoid the activity altogether.

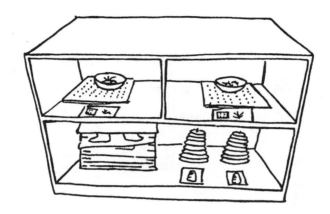

(2) Young children often find it hard to share, and table toys is one of the areas where fighting over materials can be a constant concern. One way to ease this problem is to provide duplicates. You might share with another teacher so one classroom has, for example, two stacks of rings and the other two sets of nesting boxes. (You can exchange after a few weeks and perhaps the children will be ready for one of each a few weeks after that.)

Toys that have many pieces such as pegs or beads can be divided into several small containers. Margarine tubs work very well. Then each child has his or her own toy and the need to share is reduced.

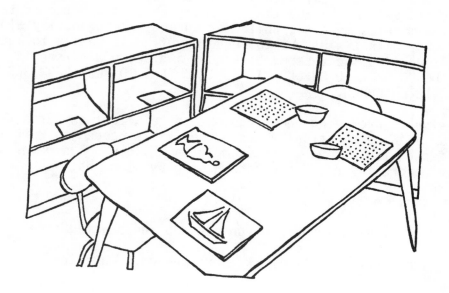

(3) If the children find it difficult to make choices, you can
select a few toys from the shelves yourself and put them out on
the table. You can even get a child started by a personal invita-
tion, perhaps saying something like: "Maybe you'd like to try
this puzzle, Mary."

IV-4. Providing encouragement and teaching skills.

Some children need a lot of encouragement to try something new.
A child who is reluctant to use table toys may be willing to go
to the area if you go too. The promise of your personal attention
for a few minutes is a powerful incentive. Just the fact that
you are there may support the child against his or her fear of
failing.

Some children need more help getting started than others. Some-
times there are cultural factors that determine whether children
are used to taking the initiative or are accustomed to waiting
for an adult to tell them what to do. Teachers of Hispanic-
American children often report that their children do not go to
the toys by themselves. The teacher needs to start them at
table toy play.

Learning to be independent, make choices, and take the initiative may be a slow process for some children. The teacher may need to help these children everyday for many weeks.

How long you need to stay with a child on any given day will depend on the child and on the toy that is being used; but often it takes only a few minutes to get a child set up and working busily alone. A child who doesn't want you to leave may find it easier to let you go if you promise to come back soon and see how he/she is doing. DO GO BACK TO CHECK. IT IS IMPORTANT TO KEEP PROMISES YOU MAKE TO CHILDREN.

In addition to providing encouragement to reluctant children, teachers may need to actually teach the skills needed to work with the different table toys. For example, a child who has never seen a puzzle before may need to be shown step by step that you

- spill out the pieces

- turn them all over so you can see the painted side

- start putting them back along the edge matching the outline

- put each piece in next to one that is there until the whole picture is made

- admire yourself for doing it!

- put it back and choose something else (or do the same one again).

Knowing how to break a task down into steps is in itself a very important skill for children to learn. Table toys are a good place to work with children on this skill. All these steps that the experienced person does without really thinking are new learnings for the beginner. And everyone is a beginner with material they haven't seen or used before.

It isn't only beginners who need support from the adults. All children thrive on encouragement. The teacher's positive attention even for a few moments can be a powerful ego boost to a young child.

IV-5. Talking with children.

Teachers can also support children by talking with them about what they are doing in the Table Toy Area. Children really enjoy showing

-40-

off their accomplishments, but teachers are very busy people. We usually feel that we should be in six or seven places at once. So we tend just to glance in the direction of the child who is calling to us and say: "Very good, Sheila." or "That's a good job, Pedro."

Positive reinforcement and praise is very important to children, but it is not enough. Children need us to talk to them -

- to give them vocabulary

- to let them know we really care about the work they do

- to teach them the names of the colors and shapes and numbers

- to help them to become more aware of what they are doing and what they are discovering

- to encourage them to talk.

Words like "good," "nice," "lovely," don't meet these needs. They don't say anything about what that child did at that time. Another way of talking to children is to use NON-JUDGEMENTAL DESCRIPTIONS. What does that mean? It means you tell the child something about what he or she is or has been doing. For example:

- "You put that whole puzzle together. It's a picture of a bear."

- "I see you are using all the red pegs."

- "You matched the two elephants. This is a giraffe. Can you find the other giraffe?"

- "I see you've put all the circles in one pile and all the squares in another pile."

- "You've lined up four cubes all in a row."

- "Your Lego tower is very tall."

Try this in your Table Toy Area: Find one sentence to say to each child about what he or she is doing that mentions at least one of these concepts:

- color(s)

- number(s)

- shape(s)

- tall/big/little

- top/bottom

- in/out/under/on top/between

- same/different.

Do the children respond as if they know that you are actually looking at their work?

When children know the names of the colors and shapes and the meaning of the numbers and size words, you can stretch their thinking when you talk to them by asking questions and making other suggestions. In this way you will often give them ideas that expand their use of the table toys - which is the subject of the next chapter.

IV-6. Summary.

Thinking back over this chapter and the ones before it, we can list some of the ways adults can help to make children's table toy play a rewarding experience. They can do this by:

- arranging the space

- selecting and displaying materials

- setting rules for the Table Toy Area

- supporting children by

  - providing encouragement
  - teaching skills
  - talking with the children.

We hope this chapter has given you some practical suggestions you will want to try out in your Table Toy Area.

Another important part of the teacher's role is structuring the use of the toys so that children continue to find them interesting, challenging, and educational. The next chapter gives suggestions for new experiences with table toys.

CHAPTER V

STRUCTURING THE USE OF TABLE TOYS

Topics in this chapter:

V-1.   Letting the children explore.

V-2.   Rotating and changing toys.

V-3.   Introducing new ways to use toys.
     (a) Verbal suggestions
     (b) Making up games
     (c) A sequence of patterning activities.

V-4.   Six multi-use table toys.
     (a) Beads and strings
     (b) Pegs and pegboards
     (c) Counting cubes
     (d) Unifix cubes
     (e) Parquetry or pattern blocks
     (f) Attribute blocks.

V-5.   Appendix - Catalogue Information.

Goals for this chapter:

1.   to explore what teachers can do to further support children in the Table Toy Area.

2.   to give teachers ideas for structuring the use of table toys to help children learn while playing.

3.   to acquaint teachers with six specific toys that are especially useful for these educational experiences.

V-1. Letting the children explore.

Children need time to explore a toy they haven't seen before: to feel
its physical properties like size and weight and shape, to study the
different colors it comes in, to discover for themselves what to do
with it. If the toy is "self-correcting" (that is: fits back together in a certain way), the children will know if they have done it
correctly. With the more open-ended type of toy like cubes, pegs,
beads or Lego, children need lots of time to experiment and try out
their own ideas.

In the previous chapter on "Supporting Children at Table Toy Play"
we were talking about children in the "free exploration" stage. The
teacher's role in helping these children is to provide encouragement,
help them get involved, teach skills when they are needed, and talk
to the children. For some children the teacher's presence may be
important just for moral support even when the children are working
on their own.

In this chapter we will focus on what to do for children who are
ready to move beyond the free exploration stage. What does the
teacher do for a child who has lost interest in the toys?

One of the best cues to help the teacher know when to intervene is
that children act bored. In fact, boredom may be the cause of some
of the problems that we listed in the first chapter. Children may
not even come to the Table Toy Area because nothing there interests
them any more. They feel they've "done it all already." If
children are using toys as weapons, that may also be a sign of
boredom. They feel that there is nothing more interesting to do
with the toys.

Even if the children aren't bored, they reach a point where they
are just doing the same thing over and over and not learning anything new. Since one of our primary goals in early childhood is to
help the children continually add to their skills and knowledge, we
have to come up with more interesting table toys or with new and
more interesting ways to use the table toys we have.

V-2. Rotating and changing the toys.

One way to rekindle interest is to offer the children something
new, to change what you have out.

If you set up the Table Toy Area for young children early in the
year (with simple toys and duplicates), you'll want to change to
more complex puzzles and more challenging toys after the children

have gotten into table toy play. Don't change everything at once; leave out toys the children still use a lot.

If you have to put everything away on Friday and set up again every Monday, as many centers do, Monday morning would be a convenient time to change some of the toys.

If your shelves were too cluttered and you put some of your toys away after seeing the pictures in Chapter III, you probably have toys in a back closet to change around.

If you don't have extra toys, try sharing with another teacher. That way children in both rooms will get the chance to try new toys. If children are not using or are misusing a toy, try putting it away for a few weeks and then bringing it out again. Children often show renewed interest in a toy if they haven't seen it for a while.

Remember to store the label with the toy so you don't have to make a new label when you bring it out again.

V-3.   Introducing new ways to use toys.

Another way to renew interest in a table toy is to invite the children to do something else with it: to introduce new activities for the children to try with the toys they have been exploring. Some toys lend themselves to a variety of uses.

In particular the "open-ended, pattern toys," described in Chapter I, Section 3, can be structured in different ways. This group includes:

- beads

- pegs

- wooden cubes

- unifix cubes

- parquetry blocks

- attribute blocks.*

The remainder of this chapter focuses on new ways to use these pattern toys.

*See V-5 for further descriptions and sources for finding these materials.

V-3. (a) <u>Verbal Suggestions</u>:

Teachers can spontaneously help children in the Table Toy Area by making suggestions or sitting for a minute or two with a child. For example, it might be appropriate to ask questions such as:

- "You've made a long train of cubes. Can you count them?"

- "What color peg are you putting in now?"

- "What shape beads are you stringing?"

If the child doesn't know the answer, you could use the moment to teach the child the color or shape name or to count with him/her. (You might want to review Chapter IV, Section 5, "Talking to Children".)

Teachers can offer suggestions:

- "That's a long train of red cubes. Can you make a blue train, too?"

- "You've got five red pegs in that row. If you put one orange peg next to each red peg, how many orange pegs would you need?"

Some children enjoy sitting with an adult and playing a kind of "follow my instructions" game like -

- "Can you make a tower with two blue cubes and two purple ones?"

- "Let's string a big, round, orange bead first. Now let's use a small, blue, square one. Can you find one for me?"

- "Put a red cube between two blue ones. Now put an orange cube on the red one."

It's easy to involve children in this activity if you call it a game. You could say to one child, "Would you like to play a game with me with these cubes?" Once you start working with one child like this, others are likely to come and ask if they can play, too.

"Follow the instructions" works well as a group activity, too. Children often like to give the instructions (language and concept development). Games like this are both fun and educational.

V-3. (b) <u>Making up games.</u>

In addition to giving verbal suggestions and playing spontaneous games, teachers can set up many different activities with these table toys. Most of these suggestions require only a little preparation by the adult. In many cases the children can work by themselves once the teacher has explained the game. The ideas on the next few pages are only a few of many possibilities. There are more suggestions in the six sections on specific materials. These ideas can also be adapted if you have other multi-use table toys and not the same ones as we describe here. We hope these suggestions will inspire you to come up with your own games and variations for your children.

(1) <u>Feeling Shapes (version I)</u> - a matching game - uses the sense of touch - teaches concept of "same" - needs an adult.

Instructions:

- Take a small cloth bag or any other type of bag which the child can reach into but not see through.

- Put a selection of beads or parquetry blocks or attribute blocks in the bag (start with two; add more as children get used to the game.)

- Give the child a bead or block to hold and feel.

- Ask the child to find (by feeling, not looking) a bead or block of the same shape inside the bag.

- The child brings out the bead or block to show and compare. Are they the same shape?

- Talk about the name of the shape and how it feels.

- Try again with a different shape.

(2) <u>Color Sorting</u> - a dividing game - uses the visual sense - teaches concept of "grouping by color" - does not need an adult.

Instructions:

- Put out a large basket of pegs or cubes or beads in different colors with a set of margarine tubs in the same colors.

- As a starter you might have only two or three colors; later as many as five if you can find the right color plastic tubs.

●   You can also vary the number of pegs (cubes, beads)
     in the larger basket.

●   Even if you don't say anything, the children will
     probably use this set of materials to sort by colors.

(3) <u>Feeling Shapes (version II)</u> - a shape recognition game -
uses the sense of touch - tests knowledge of shape names - needs
an adult.

Instructions:

●   For this game use only beads or parquetry or
     attribute blocks that have a clearly recognizable
     shape such as "round," "square," "egg-shaped"
     ("oval").

●   Be sure the child you are playing with knows these
     shapes and their names.

●   Put a selection in the bag.

●   Ask the child to find the shape you name (by
     feeling, not looking).

(4) <u>More and Less</u> - a counting game - uses the visual sense -
reinforces understanding of concepts of "more," "less" - two
players - needs an adult only if children don't yet know the
meaning of "more," "less."

Preparation: Make a spinner: On a square piece of cardboard, draw
a diagonal line between corners. This divides the square in half.
Label one half "MORE," and the other half "LESS." Cover with clear
adhesive-backed (Contact) paper for durability. For a sturdy
spinner, mount the cardboard on a square of scrap wood. Make a
wide cardboard arrow - cover it too with clear adhesive-backed
paper. Punch a hole in the arrow and attach the arrow and card to
the board with a nail at the center.

Instructions:

●   Each player chooses a color
     and gets 20 objects (pegs,
     beads, cubes, unifix cubes).

●   At each turn, both players put
     out any number from zero to
     five.

-48-

- Adult asks, "Who put out more?" "Who put out less?"

- One player spins (children can take turns spinning).

- If the arrow stops on LESS, child with less out takes all that are out.

- If the arrow stops on MORE, child with more out wins all that are out.

- Continue until one child wins all.

- Divide pieces (out) again and start over.

(5) <u>Following Instructions</u> - good for language development - best with older fours and fives.

Instructions:

- Give each person the same set of materials (cubes or pegs of different colors or a string and some beads or a set of attribute blocks).

- Have each person put a screen in front of them (a box top works well) so no one else can see what they are making and they can't see what anyone else is doing.

- Make a pattern piece by piece telling the children what you are doing with each piece.

- The others are supposed to do exactly the same as you are doing.

- Take down the screens and see if everyone's pattern came out the same. If they are different, talk about what happened.

- Let the children take turns giving the instructions.

V-3. (c) <u>A sequence of patterning activities</u>:

A whole series of patterning activities can be made up for any of these toys (pegs, beads, cubes, parquetry blocks). These lead the child from random designs to complex patterns and help develop reading readiness skills in particular. Many of these activities require some preparation by the adult but the children can work on them alone. We'll use the stringing beads as an example, but

-49-

all of these activities can also be done with pegs, colored cubes, unifix cubes and parquetry blocks.

Instructions:

- Step 1: The children explore the toy. They make several "necklaces" or designs over a period of time.

- Step 2: One day you say, "I like your design. I'm going to try to make one just like it." and you do so, describing each bead or cube or block you put on. The child gets the idea that a pattern can be copied and is usually quite pleased that you were interested in his/hers.

- Step 3: You make a pattern in beads on a string or in cubes on the table. You can mount a string of beads on a card. Suggest that the child make one just like yours. This is a three dimensional pattern the child is copying because it is made with real beads or cubes. You can make any kind of pattern (all one shape or alternating shapes or all one color or alternating colors) but keep

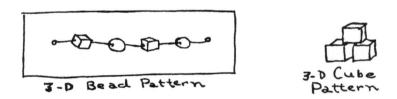

3-D Bead Pattern   3-D Cube Pattern

it simple at the beginning. You can use one child's pattern for other children to copy.

- Step 4: Cut out paper forms that match the color and shape of the beads, cubes, or blocks. Cut strips (3" x 12" is a convenient size) from white cardboard. Keep them handy in a box. When the child has made an interesting pattern, ask if he/she would like to make a picture of it with you. Find the right colors and shapes in the box and paste them onto a card in the order the child did on the string or table. (You can also just draw it on with crayons.)

  If you describe what you are doing to the child as you do it, you are also fostering language development and making the child feel more included in the activity.

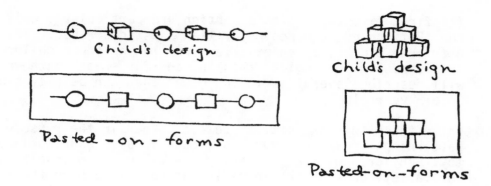

Child's design

Pasted-on-forms

Child's design

Pasted-on-forms

Making pictures of a child's pattern may also make it easier for the child to be willing to undo the beads or design at clean-up time. This step shows the child how a three-dimensional physical object can be represented in a two-dimensional picture. Children often want to use the paper forms themselves to make their own pictures from the beads they have strung or the designs they have made.

Step 5: With crayons or the paper forms make patterns of cards for the child to follow. This is the same as step 3 but at a more advanced level. (For this stage only, there are commercially available pattern cards for some of this material.) You can do this at many levels. You can ask the child to make a complete string that copies yours or you can start a pattern and ask the child to keep it going (much more difficult than just copying). The first patterns could be all the same type of bead or block. Then you might alternate two beads or colors of blocks and so on. At this stage you can make beads interesting even to five and six-year-olds by setting up complex patterns or designs.

V-4. Six multi-use table toys.

This section will cover in more detail the six sets of early childhood materials involved in the games and activities just described. All of these toys can be used for developing intellectual skills in young children. They were chosen because many centers have them. While you may have other "open-ended pattern type" materials, the patterns and games shown here can be applied to other toys as well.

The first five toys in this section are particularly well suited for the "Patterning Sequence Activities" just described. The sixth, Attribute Blocks, is an excellent way to introduce children to the skills needed for logical thinking and for school mathemetics. We will describe several beginning games that can be played by and with 3 to 5 year olds.

While these toys are similar to each other in their usefulness for patterning (grouping, ordering), each is also a uniquely different toy. Children will enjoy having several of them to play with both for variety and for the special features of each of these materials.

V-4. (a) <u>Beads and Strings</u>

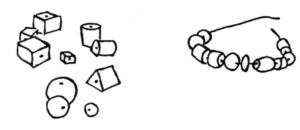

<u>Material:</u>

beads of various sizes, shapes, colors, with holes through them and strings.

<u>Special Features:</u>

- eye-hand control

- small muscle development

- 3-dimensional shapes (cubes and pegs come in only one shape, pattern blocks and attribute blocks are flatter)

- reading in sequence

<u>Free Exploration Time</u>: Children are likely to -

- string beads in arbitrary order
- line beads up on table
- try to make circles, cylinders stand up
- sort by color or shape
- string beads in a pattern.

<u>Vocabulary Building</u>: Can be used to teach -

- color names
- shape names
- counting.

<u>Enrichment Activities</u>: Some suggestions might be -

- Feeling Shapes Games
- Color Sorting Game
- More/Less Game
- Following Instructions Game
- The Pattern Sequence.

V-4. (b) <u>Pegs and Pegboards</u>

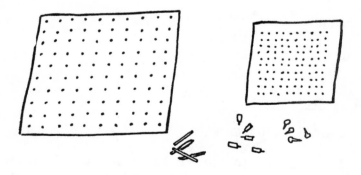

Material:

sticks in various colors, boards with 25 or 100 holes to hold
sticks upright (both come in various sizes and materials).
Pegboards come in small (6" square), large (10" square) and
jumbo (16" - 24" square). You need different pegs for
different size boards.

Special Features:

- eye-hand coordination

- making pictures/designs

- patterns

- arithmetic

- small muscle development

- one-to-one correspondence.

Free Exploration: Children are likely to -

- fill up the whole board with different colored
  pegs

- make their own color patterns

- make designs.

Vocabulary Building: Can be used to teach -

- color names

- next to/between

- down

- across.

Enrichment Activities:

- Color Sorting Game

- Ditto Sheets to record patterns made. Instead of cards
  for patterns you can make ditto sheets that look like a

pegboard. Keep a set of colored pencils (in the colors of the pegs) handy so you can fill in the pattern a child makes.

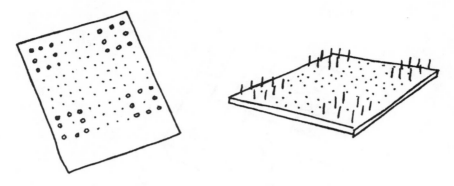

See if the children can transfer their pegboard pattern to a ditto sheet by themselves.

Help the very young child learn to make a pattern step by step. Fill in only one circle on a ditto sheet. On another sheet fill in the same circle plus one for the next peg in the pattern. Continue adding only one peg per sheet. Staple together in order to make a "Build a Pattern Book."

● Arithmetic Games

(1) Ask child to put one peg in first row, two in second, adding one more for each row. Have child count pegs in each row. Look at step design made by pegs.

(2) Give the child addition problems like put one red peg and two blue pegs in first row. Fill second row with yellow pegs until it is just as long as first. How many yellow pegs did you use?

This is the beginning of the concept of "sets" basic to math.

V-4. (c) <u>Colored Cubes</u>

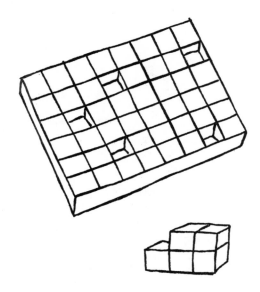

<u>Material</u>:

hardwood cubes, 1" on each side, 6 or 9 colors, 96 to 120 in a box.

<u>Special Features of this Material</u>:

- spatial relations

- balance

- reading readiness patterns

- dramatic play

- one-to-one correspondence.

<u>Free Exploration Time</u>: You may see children -

- line them up as trains

- build towers

- make buildings

- sort by color

- put in box by color

- build bridges

- make designs.

Vocabulary Building: Can be used to teach -

- color names

- space words: on top of/ under/between/in front of/ behind....

- longer/shorter

- higher/lower

- more/less

- counting

- one-to-one correspondence.

Enrichment Activities: Some suggestions might be -

- Color Sorting Game

- More/Less Game

- Pattern Sequence Games

    (1) Matching the pattern by putting the cubes directly on the card is easier than repro-ducing the pattern on the table next to the card.

    (2) Patterns which suggest outlines of letters develop reading readiness skills.

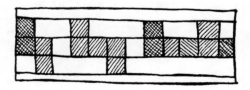

card #15 for "My Dog Barks" (from Develop-mental Learning Materials)

(3) Three-dimensional patterns in perspective are
     a special feature of cubes.

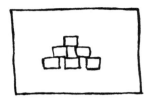   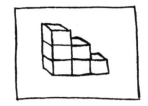

flat design   perspective design

Books:

A useful activity book for colored cubes is Patterns by William
McKillip, Practical Paper #32, University of Georgia, December,
1969, 45 pp. available from ERIC system #ED077690.

V-4. (d) Unifix Cubes

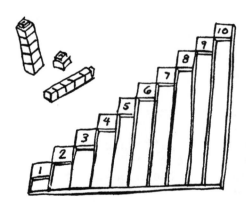

Material:

plastic cubes that snap together, variety of colors, accessories for
development of math concepts are also available.

Special Features of this Material:

- counting

- mathematical relationships

- because they snap together, trains made of unifix cubes can be lifted up and carried around (unlike the colored inch cubes)

- small muscle development

- one-to-one correspondence.

Free Exploration Time: Children are likely to -

- build long trains (on floor)

- build tall towers (on table)

- make observations of measurements
  - "This is as long as the box."
  - "This is as tall as I am."

Vocabulary Building: Can be used to teach -

- color names

- numbers, counting

- taller/shorter

- higher/lower

- longer/shorter

- more/less.

Enrichment Activities: Some suggestions might be -

- Color Sorting Game

- More/Less Game

- Number Towers - use unifix cubes for showing children simple arithmetic facts - equivalence, addition, steps from one to ten, etc. (See under Pegs, Arithmetic Games (2), page 55).

● Pattern Trains (like the pattern sequence) by using different combinations of colors in different numbers, you can make patterns for children to copy or continue:

a two color alternating pattern - fairly easy

two of color A and one of color B - more difficult pattern

one of color A, two of color B, three of color C - still more difficult pattern.

● New Patterns From Old - this is an advanced game in which children discover new facts about repeating patterns - adults might enjoy trying it themselves.

Make a three color pattern.

Make the same pattern 10 times and attach them together in one long line.

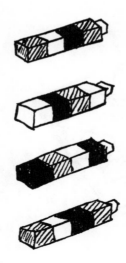

Start at the beginning of the chain; count four
cubes, break the chain, continue to break the
chain after every four cubes, putting the sections in front of each other on the table.

What do you see happening now?

V-4. (e) Parquetry or Pattern Blocks

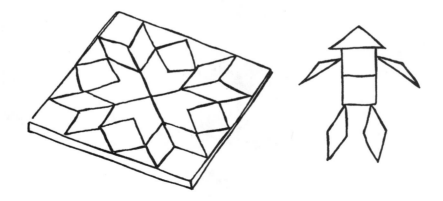

Material:

flat wooden, plastic or rubber pieces of assorted geometric shapes and colors.

Special Features of this Material:

- diamond shapes

- half shapes (2 triangles = square) or (2 triangles = diamond)

- spatial orientation (turning piece may make it fit pattern

- small pieces and more shapes provide more variety than cubes for older children

- open pattern designs can be very challenging

- develops visual perception of shape, size, area

- mirror images

- different perspectives.

<u>Free Exploration Time</u>: You may see children -

- make designs

- stand them up

- sort by color

- sort by shape

- pile up by shape.

<u>Vocabulary Building</u>: Can be used to teach -

- color names

- shape names

<u>Enrichment Activities</u>: Some suggestions might be -

- Feeling Shapes Games

- Lotto Game - to familiarize children with shapes you can make a lotto board and cards. Take two pieces of cardboard. Divide one into sections, cut the other into matching pieces. Paste a colored paper or colored adhesive-backed (Contact) paper shape to each section of the large board and an identical color-shape to one of the smaller pieces. Laminate or cover each piece of cardboard with clear adhesive-backed (Contact) paper.

- Pattern Sequence as with other toys in this group. To make your own Design Cards, cut out colored paper shapes to match parquetry pieces.

    (1) When children make a "building" or design, offer to put pattern on paper.

    (2) Make real object model for children to copy, have children copy each others', teacher offers to copy children's.

    (3) Make pattern cards with the colored paper shapes as with cubes or beads.

         The same card can be used at different

levels of difficulty:

- match by placing blocks on cards

- copy by remaking pattern on table
  next to card

- copy from other side of table (perspective difference)

- make pattern as it would look in a
  mirror to check self).

The cards can be made increasingly complex.

- very simple -- one block, two in a row:

- simple figures with each block drawn in
  color and shape:

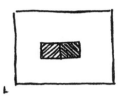

- figures with shapes outlined but not
  colored:

- outline of figure only:

- Parquetry blocks are particularly good for the "Following
  Instructions" Game because the shapes can be used to make
  "houses," "people" or elaborate designs.

-64-

● Parquetry block pictures can be representational, and therefore you could think of designs that would particularly appeal to your group of children. For a complex picture like this one, you might want to sort out the necessary pieces, put them in a plastic cup or can, and have them available with the picture.

Picture of a parrot made with ESS pattern blocks.

V-4. (f) Attribute Blocks

Material:

60 plastic pieces (that vary by shape, color, size, and thickness); the five shapes are circles, squares, rectangles, triangles and hexagons. Manuals for using the blocks are available.

Special Features of this Material:

- classification

- sorting

- readiness for mathematics ("sets").

Free Exploration Time: Children are likely to -

- feel them and look at them

- put them back into box (this is like a puzzle because the box is molded so each shape fits only in a partic- ular place)

- create buildings and designs

- begin to sort by color or shape or make patterns like putting each small block on top of the corresponding big block.

Vocabulary Building: Can be used to teach -

- shape names - "circle," "square," "rectangle," "triangle," "hexagon"

- color names - "red," "yellow," "blue"

- large/small

- thick/thin.

Teachers should encourage and help children to describe blocks by all four names. "You have the large, thick, blue square."

Related Activities:

In conjunction with the Attribute Blocks, you can help children to be more aware of shapes in the world around them by putting up pictures from magazines of real objects like a square cracker, an apple cut in half, etc.

Enrichment Activities: Some suggestions might include -

- Lotto Game: cut out shapes from colored paper or red/blue/yellow adhesive-backed (Contact) paper.

Glue them onto a board.

(1) Match actual pieces to the board.

(2) Make individual shape cards in same way
     as large card. Match as in a lotto game.

(3) Combine with the "feeling shapes" game.
     Put blocks in a container, child decides
     which shape he/she needs and tries to
     find it by touch.

(4) Use with dice (see below) and something
     to cover squares. Roll three dice (ones
     indicating color, size and shape). Anyone
     who has that block covers that space. Con-
     tinue until all the cards are filled in
     (that way you will have all winners -
     first winner, second winner, etc.).

● Cards: Make a card for each feature (12 in all - 5 shapes)
  3 colors, large/small, thick/thin). You might use stick
  figures for the size and thick/thin lines for thickness.
  Children can match cards with blocks and the cards can be
  used with the ropes and the grid (see below).

● Strings:

(1) Put out circles made of red, blue, yellow yarn
     saying something like, "Here are some strings.
     What can you do with them?" The children will
     probably sort by color.

(2) Do same but with thick and thin strings.

(3) Put out neutral color strings (yarn) and a
     feature card for each. The children will
     probably sort to match the feature.

● <u>Grid Pattern</u>: Make a 3" x 4" grid on the table with masking tape.

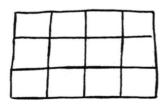
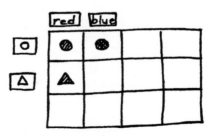

(1) Suggest that children use it with the blocks. Children may line blocks up in a pattern or stack one group in a box. USE DESCRIPTIVE STATEMENTS (Chapter IV-5) to point out to the children the patterns or groupings they have made.

(2) Use the feature cards to name each line and row of grid. Children can fill in grid with blocks.

● <u>Dice</u>: You can use counting cubes to make the dice. Glue onto each side of the cube a piece of paper with one of the possible choices for that feature. You need four cubes:

     size: you can use stick figures to show large and small

     shapes: one shape will go on two sides

     color: red, yellow, blue

     thickness: thick and thin lines.

(1) Start with one color and one shape, e.g. put out all the circles so each can be seen. Give a child the color cube. Child gets to keep a circle of the color he/she throws.

(2) Add more dice and pieces as children get adept at the game, until children are using all the dice and the whole Attribute Blocks set.

(3) Child shakes out cubes, lines them up, reads them off, finds block that matches and keeps it until game is over.

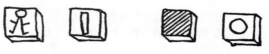

e.g.   large   thin   red   circle

(4) Child picks a block and then lines up dice so block is described.

(5) Time children with a sand timer. (The last two versions were invented by children. Let your children make up their own versions.)

● Children invent games. After you've played some of these games, the children may want to use the blocks alone. See what they do with them now. For example, one child made an elaborate pattern with all the thin blocks and then made the same pattern again with the thick blocks.

● Older children who have had a lot of experience with attribute blocks may be ready to get into even more elaborate games. The Guide books have suggestions for these. Other useful articles include:

CRUIKSHANK, DOUGLAS. "Sorting, Classifying, and Logic." The Arithmetic Teacher 21 (Nov., 1974): 588-598.

DENMAN, THERESA. "Mathematics the 'Attribute Game'." Instructor 83 (Nov., 1973): 51-52.

V-5. Appendix: Catalogue Information.

The following six companies are among the major manufacturers
and suppliers of educational table toys for young children. All
of the toys discussed in this chapter can be found in one or more
of these catalogues.

Some toys (like beads and pegs) are available from all these
sources, but prices, quantity, material and style may vary.
Other toys (in particular, unifix cubes and attribute blocks)
are only sold by a few companies (Childcraft, Kaplan).

This list is not exhaustive. It is possible that there are other
companies that make similar materials. These toys may also be
available through other school supply companies that sell from
several manufacturers. If you write for catalogues from these
six companies, however, you will find the toys and games discussed in this Manual.

- Some Manufacturers and Suppliers of Table Toys:

  Childcraft Education Corporation
  20 Kilmer Road
  Edison, New Jersey 08817

  Developmental Learning Materials (DLM)
  7440 Natachez Avenue
  Niles, Illinois 60648

  Ideal School Supply Company
  1100 South Lavergne Avenue
  Oak Lawn, Illinois 60453

  Kaplan School Supply Corporation
  600 Jonestown Road
  Winston-Salem, North Carolina 27103

  Milton-Bradley/Playskool
  Springfield, Massachusetts 01101

  For parquetry (pattern blocks), an excellent source is:

  Elementary Science Study (ESS)
  Education Development Center, Inc.
  55 Chapel Street
  Newton, Massachusetts 02160.

o   Pattern Cards - In V-3 (c) we discussed the value of having
      cards with patterns for children to follow and use with
      these table toys. You can make your own cards quite easily
      for whatever set you have, but if you want to buy cards it
      might be useful to consider the availability of pattern
      cards when you are comparing different manufacturers'
      materials.

      Sometimes the pattern cards from one company can be used
      with a different set of materials, but sometimes card
      sets are not interchangeable. For example:

      For beads - DLM and Ideal make cards, but each company's
      pattern cards can only be used with that company's beads
      because each set has different shapes and sizes.

      For pegs - the DLM and Ideal pattern cards can be used
      with any 6 color peg set. The 6 colors are red, orange,
      yellow, green, blue and purple.

      For counting cubes - DLM cards can be used with any of
      the six color sets.

      For parquetry blocks - the DLM Large Parquetry Design
      Cards can be used with the Playskool Parquetry Blocks.
      Ideal also makes cards for its Tactilmat (rubber) par-
      quetry pieces. ESS has activity books for its pattern
      blocks (which are quite different from the other par-
      quetry sets).

CHAPTER VI

MAKING YOUR OWN TABLE TOYS

Topics covered in this chapter:

Goals for this chapter:

1.   to think about reasons for making rather than
          buying table toys.

2.   in particular, to think about the importance of
          having materials that reflect a variety of racial
          and cultural groups, and that show men and women
          in similar roles.

3.   to get instructions for making a wide variety of
          inexpensive educational table toys.

VI-1. Why make your own table toys?

Many teachers make table toys to add to their store-bought
selection. Some of the reasons teachers make their own materials
include:

- Money

    - "I have only a small budget to buy table toys."

    - "I can get more toys for less if I make them."

- Satisfaction

    - "I feel good when I see the children use a toy
      I've made."

    - "I enjoy the idea of making useful toys out of
      scrap materials or throwaways."

- Getting Exactly What You Want

    - "I can make a game to go along with whatever I
      want the children to learn about: numbers, or
      shapes, or different animals..."

    - "There aren't enough commercial materials that
      show Black and Spanish people, so I make my own."

    - "I wanted my children to see women and men in
      nonsexist pictures, so I found some and made my
      own puzzles from them."

These last two statements are so important that we ought to stop
and think about them.

VI-2. Racism and sexism in table toys.

Young children are visually oriented. They can't yet read words
but pictures make a very deep impression on them. At the same time,
young children are sorting out information about the world they live

in - who does what, who is important, who should they try to be like. A lot of this information comes to children in the pictures they see.

When young children see pictures in lotto games where all the people are White, they get the message that only White people count, that no one else is important. This message is harmful to ALL children - to Black, Hispanic, Native American, Oriental and other children who don't see people like themselves in the pictures because it reinforces the notion that all those fun things to do and be are not for them; and to White children because it teaches them that they alone can grow up to be like the people in the pictures they see, that other people are not as important.

Have you ever really looked at the pictures on your table toys? You might want to try this method. Take out all your table toys that have pictures on them: lotto games, puzzles, community workers, etc. Look carefully at the pictures.

Are all the people White?

If there are Black people, do they look like Black people you've seen? Do they look like White people with colored in faces? Do they all look the same?

What are the White people doing? What are the Black people doing? Are they in less important or less interesting activities than White people.

You could go through the same set of questions substituting "Hispanic," "Oriental," "Native American" ... for "Black." Don't forget to look at your puzzles too, especially if you have some old ones. The little Indian boy in feather headdress may be "cute," but if your children think that he is typical of the way Native American children generally dress, they have gotten a stereotyped message that is demeaning to a whole group of people.

In addition to looking at images of racial and ethnic groups in your table toys, you should also think about your toys and similar questions with regard to sex roles:

Are all the people men?

If there are women, what are they doing?

Are women shown only in traditional jobs - mommy, teacher, nurse?

Are the men doing active, courageous type activities? Are the women passive - watching?

-74-

Messages in pictures have a tremendous impact on young children. Have you ever heard a boy in your classroom tell a girl, "No, you have to be the nurse, girls can't be doctors "? A lotto game or community workers set with pictures of men as doctors and women as nurses strongly reinforces that sexist idea and helps close future doors for that girl even before she has gotten to first grade.

You can change the messages these children have been getting by not keeping racist and sexist table toys in your classroom. You can instead offer your children table toys that have pictures of both men and women in nontraditional roles and have pictures of people from different racial and ethnic backgrounds doing equally important and fun activities.

There is still very little nonracist and nonsexist material available from companies for early childhood table toys. Some good sources might include:

Women's Action Alliance 370 Lexington Avenue, New York, New York 10017 - a set of cardboard community workers figures that are nonracist as well as nonsexist; also information on nonsexist curriculum; some of these materials are available from Milton-Bradley Company.

Developmental Learning Materials, 7440 Natchez Avenue, Niles, Illinois 60648 - some Spanish materials, puzzles and posters of Hispanic people.

The best and least expensive solution to the problem of getting nonracist and nonsexist table toys is to make your own. In the rest of this chapter there are many examples which we hope will inspire you. These are mostly made by using photographs and magazine pictures. One additional advantage to this source is that these are pictures of real people. In this way you can show children a much greater variety of people than they are likely to see in manufactured toys and games.

Time as well as money is limited for all of us. One solution is to involve parents in an evening of making toys for the classroom. While hands are busy cutting and pasting, informal discussions on the materials, their use and the learning anticipated can take place.

VI-3. Lotto games.

In a lotto game there is one big card with several sections and smaller cards to match each section of the large card. Lotto games develop

- visual perception/discrimination

- matching

- one-to-one correspondence

- recognition of letters, numbers, objects (whatever the game is about).

Some examples:

- A numbers lotto board. (Lotto used to reinforce a particular learning concept.)

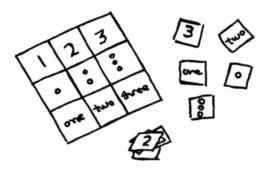

- Vinyl paper patterns. This is made from scraps of different patterns of adhesive backed paper (e.g. Contact paper). Lotto can be easy or difficult depending on how different the pictures are. Pictures or patterns that are very similar require more developed perceptual skills. A board with many bright patterns may look good mounted on a larger size plain board.

To make lotto games: Take two identical pieces of cardboard. (The backs of writing pads are a good source of free cardboard.) Line both pieces in the same way into as many sections as you want. Leave one whole. Cut the other up. Draw or paste identical pictures onto one small card and one section of the large card. To make paper games more durable, laminate the cards or cover with clear adhesive-backed paper. Keep the small cards together with a rubber band.

To get two copies of the same picture, use two identical catalogues, magazines, workbooks, sheets of sticker pictures or stamps, or draw them yourself.

VI-4. Flip books.

A ring binder can be used to make a matching toy.

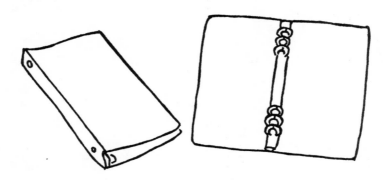

A convenient size for young children to work with is a small binder that measures 7" long, 4 1/2" across the front and has six small rings inside. It can be bought at a five-and-ten or stationery store for about a dollar.

To make the matching game that goes inside, cut cardboard or oaktag into cards that fit inside the book. For identical matches, cut cards to go over three of the six rings. Make two copies of each picture. Laminate or cover each card with clear adhesive-backed paper. Punch holes so the cards fit into the book. Put each set in a different order.

-77-

The child chooses the picture to be matched in one set of cards
and flips through the other set until the matching picture appears.
Four pictures might be a good number for very young children. A
book for older children might have as many as ten choices. Keeping
all the pictures to a theme (birds, transportation, numbers, houses,
letters, people, flowers ...) would make the activity a more mean-
ingful learning experience for children.

Some examples:

- Birds (a simple game)

binder open to first cards   binder open to matching cards

- Patterns (a more difficult game)

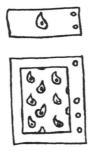

> This example uses one set of large cards (4 holes) and
> one set of smaller cards (2 holes). Each large card is
> covered with a different pattern of adhesive backed
> paper. You can include the same pattern in different
> color combinations. Each small card shows just a part
> of the corresponding large card pattern. This "part-
> to-whole" matching is an advanced perception game.

-78-

The binder keeps all the cards together and is itself a durable container for storing the cards.

VI-5. Puzzles.

Puzzles help to build perceptual skills like lotto games and flip books with the added complication that each small piece is only part of the larger picture. Puzzles can make children think about the whole (person or object) and its parts.

Homemade puzzles are an excellent way to introduce culturally relevant materials into your classroom. Use photographs of the children, their families, familiar scenes, etc. Another source would be pictures from magazines. National Geographic often has beautiful pictures of different ethnic groups. Ebony or Essence would have pictures of Black people.

You can use black and white or color photos or pictures, but you should choose ones that clearly show just one or two people or an uncomplicated scene so that it does not become too diffi-cult for young children to complete the puzzle.

To make puzzles: Mount the photo or picture on cardboard. Cut into sections. (Puzzles do not have to have inter-locking, jigsawed edges. Straight cuts are fine.) Dry-mount and laminate or cover each piece with clear adhesive-backed paper.

Some examples:

- Native American (from National Geographic magazine)

● A Black couple (from <u>Ebony</u> magazine)

To make very simple matching puzzles, use two copies of the same photograph or picture. Two copies of the same issue of a magazine will give you duplicate pictures. Mount one copy whole. Cut the other copy into two or three parts.

If you have only one copy of the photo or picture, but you want to give the children a little help in getting it together properly, you can line a piece of blank cardboard to show where the pieces go. The cardboard should be the exact size of the finished puzzle.

You don't have to have a frame for each puzzle, but you can make a cardboard one quite easily. Measure the completed puzzle. Find or cut a piece of cardboard about 1 1/2" to 2" all the way around with other strips of cardboard. Paint the raised edging or cover with solid color adhesive-backed paper.

VI-6. Spool boards.

Several interesting toys can be made from scrap wood, empty thread spools and wooden dowels. Collect thread spools from parents, buy them from a hobby shop, or ask a tailor or seamstress to save them for you. Wooden dowels come in many thicknesses and are sold inexpensively in lumber stores.

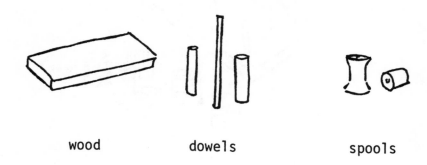

wood   dowels   spools

Spool boards develop manual dexterity - small muscle control. They can reinforce different concepts depending on how you set them up.

To make a spool board: Take a thick block of wood (a rectangular shape works well). Mark in pencil where you want each dowel to go. Drill holes for each dowel. The size hole you drill will depend on the thickness of the dowel.) Cut the dowel to the desired length, just enough for the number of spools you want to go on that piece. Glue in each dowel. Put the spools on.

Some examples:

● Color matching toy: Paint each spool in a different color. Use the same colors to paint circles on the wood around each dowel.

● Grouping by patterns: Make rows of three all along the board. Separate spools into groups of three and put a different design on each group. You can paint designs on or use different patterns of adhesive-backed paper. If you have different size spools within each group, this toy will be even more challenging. The designs don't have to be very artistic, only clearly different from each other.

Mark the board with the pattern around the dowel so
the children will know where each spool goes.

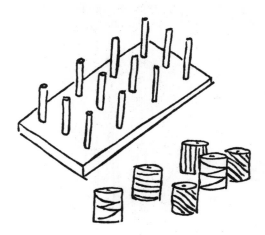

- Ordering by size: If you use dowels and spools of
  different sizes, you can make a matching or grouping
  game where the child learns that a bigger spool needs
  a thicker rod to sit on.

- Counting: a numbers board. By varying the height of
  the dowel you put in the board, you also vary the
  number of spools that will fit on that dowel. To make
  a numbers board, set it up so that the first dowel
  will hold just one spool; the second, two; and so on.
  If you use the same size spools throughout, this is
  a very graphic way of letting children see how each
  number means adding one to the number you had
  before. Each tower is one spool higher than the
  one before.

"a numbers board"

spool board exam-
ple #4

• A two size number board: You can make a more
  advanced toy that combines the concepts of the
  last two examples. Put in two rows of five dowels;
  one row that takes small thin spools and another
  that takes larger, thicker spools. In each row
  the child has to build towers one to five spools
  high. Within the same row, each tower is one spool
  higher than the one before, but the two "four spool"
  towers are not the same height, even though they
  have the same number of spools on them. This helps
  teach children "conservation of number," you can
  have the same number in two piles even though
  one pile looks bigger.

VI-7. Sorting games.

Among the basic learning skills that three to five-year-olds should
be practicing are categorization, counting, and the beginning of
letter/sound recognition. Any of these can be reinforced in a game
where the children have to sort pictures into different groups.
Here are three ways to set up sorting games.

• Shoebox, clothespins and cards:

  Divide the inside of a shoebox into as many compartments
  as you want by gluing in cardboard pieces. Cut slots in
  the top of the shoebox so that each slot feeds into one
  of the compartments. Label each slot by putting a letter,
  number, or picture on a clothespin and clipping that
  clothespin to a slot. For the cards: Draw or cut out
  pictures and mount on cardboard. Be sure the cardboard
  cards will fit easily in the slots. There should be
  several cards that go in each compartment.

  In the picture example which follows, there are twenty-
  five cards - there are five different pictures and
  five cards of each picture with one to five items on a
  card.

Example: a shoebox number sorting game, one to five.

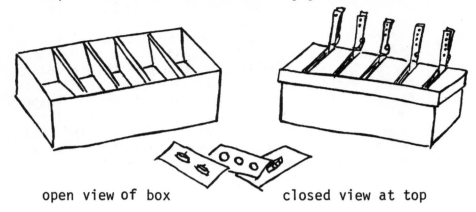

open view of box   closed view at top

● Open front box:

A different kind of sorting box can be made by finding or making an open faced compartmented holder that looks like this:

This example of a homemade box was constructed by taping pieces of cardboard together. You can make as many sections as you want. Make cards to be sorted and label the sections appropriately. There are two advantages to this box over the closed shoe box:

- you can use larger cards

- the children can see the cards they have already sorted.

This arrangement can be used to sort cards on any topic. Our example is of a "fabric pattern sorter." Each card

-84-

measures 5" x 6" and is a piece of cardboard covered
with a piece of scrap material.

● __Grouping on a board:__

Take a large piece of cardboard or posterboard. Line
it off both horizontally and vertically into sections.
At the top of each column put a picture to label that
group. Make small cards to fit onto each section of
the board. Use a juice can or other recycled container
to store the small cards. Label the can and the board
with some identifying picture so they will be put away
together.

Example: Nature picture grouping board.

the board   some cards

This game uses gummed stamps that have been mounted on
cardboard and covered with clear adhesive-backed paper.
The children have to place all the different flower
cards in the row with the flower on top, all the bird
pictures in the bird row, etc. There are just enough
small cards to fill each space on the board.

Any one of these three examples could be adapted to many different
sorting games. To make the cards to be sorted, you can use

● your own drawings

● reading and math workbooks (including the kind
you can buy in variety stores and supermarkets)

● pads/packets of gummed picture stickers

- scrap material

- stamps (National Wildlife stamps include great pictures of birds, animals, flowers, fish, butterflies, etc.).

ADDITIONAL RESOURCES FOR THE CREATIVE CURRICULUM

Teacher Competencies Related to the Four Curriculum Manuals

The Child Development Associate (CDA) National office has outlined six competency areas for teachers of young children. These competency areas specify those skills needed in establishing and maintaining a proper child-care environment, in nurturing children's physical, social, emotional and intellectual growth, and in promoting good relations between parents and the child development center. The workshops on which the Creative Curriculum was based, were designed to help teachers develop specific competencies for the CDA credential. Sample behaviors were outlined to show that a teacher was skillful in each of the CDA competency areas as they related to the classroom area being addressed: Blocks, House Corner, Table Toys or Art. The list of CDA-related competencies for each of the four classroom areas addressed in the Creative Curriculum is now available from Creative Associates.

Room Arrangement as a Teaching Strategy

"Room Arrangement as a Teaching Strategy," an audiovisual training package consists of a 25 minute filmstrip, cassette narrative and illustrated booklet. The filmstrip shows how the classroom environment affects children's behavior and how the arrangement of furniture and materials can support a teacher's goals for children - individually and in a group. The booklet includes the complete narrative with drawings of 88 slides, suggestions for trainers on presenting the filmstrip in a workshop, and a list of references. The cassette is available in both Spanish and English. Designed for center directors and trainers to use with teachers and parents, the package highlights the Curriculum's major principles and sets the stage for the Creative Curriculum.

Technical Assistance and Training

Creative Associates Inc. staff are early childhood specialists who have worked with and provided training to programs across the country. The staff provides training for teachers, center directors and other trainers and offers workshops on a variety of topics, including:

- Implementing the Creative Curriculum
- Training of Trainers
- Bilingual Education
- Nutrition Education

For information on obtaining these resources, please write or call:

Creative Associates, Inc.
3201 New Mexico Avenue, N.W.
Suite 270
Washington, D.C. 20016
(202) 966-5804